Ho! Ho! Ho!

Ho! Ho! Ho!

A Stockingful of Christmas Cartoons

Edited by S. Gross
and Jim Charlton

BARNES
&NOBLE
BOOKS
NEW YORK

1998 Barnes & Noble Books

ISBN 0-7607-0777-4

Printed in Mexico.

98 99 00 01 02 M 9 8 7 6 5 4 3 2 1

"It means that Santa's coming to town."

"All of our officers are busy right now. Would you care to request a carol instead?"

"Now hand me the angel!"

"That, of course, was 'Jingle Bells' . . . our next selection will be 'I Heard the Bells on Christmas Day' . . ."

"We're just pleased he can still get into the Christmas spirit."

"Oh, oh — here comes the Yule tide!"

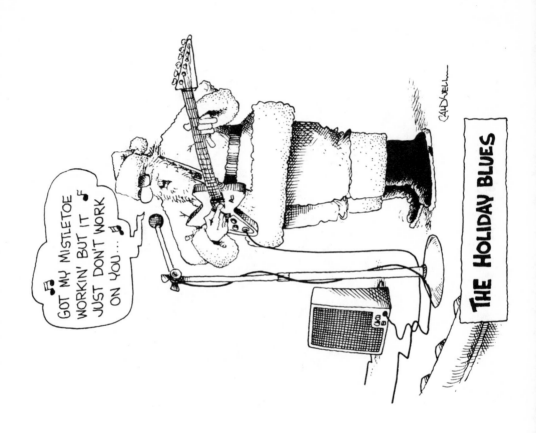

"Is Margie's Yule Log getting bigger every year, or are we getting smaller?"

"Dad, Fax this out to Santa for me."

MEET SANTA'S ENTOURAGE

Larry B. ~ his accountant

"Looks like he's going to have a mighty good year!"

Marge Z. ~ his lawyer

"I love him like a son."

Lorna R. ~ his hairdresser

"Santa's hair is surprisingly fine."

Gerald M. ~ his tailor

"One year, it's buttons, the next year it's no buttons. One year, it's a 5-inch-wide belt, the next year it's gotta be 3½ inches. One year, it's..."

Barney G. ~ his agent and P.R. man

"I'm sorry, but Santa always gets 50% of the gross."

Mrs. Claus ~ his wife and confidante

"He's really a very sweet man."

R. Chast

"You promise, but can you deliver?"

"Try spreading them out a little bit more."

'MESSIAH' SING-ALONG FOR TODAY'S PERSON-ON-THE-GO

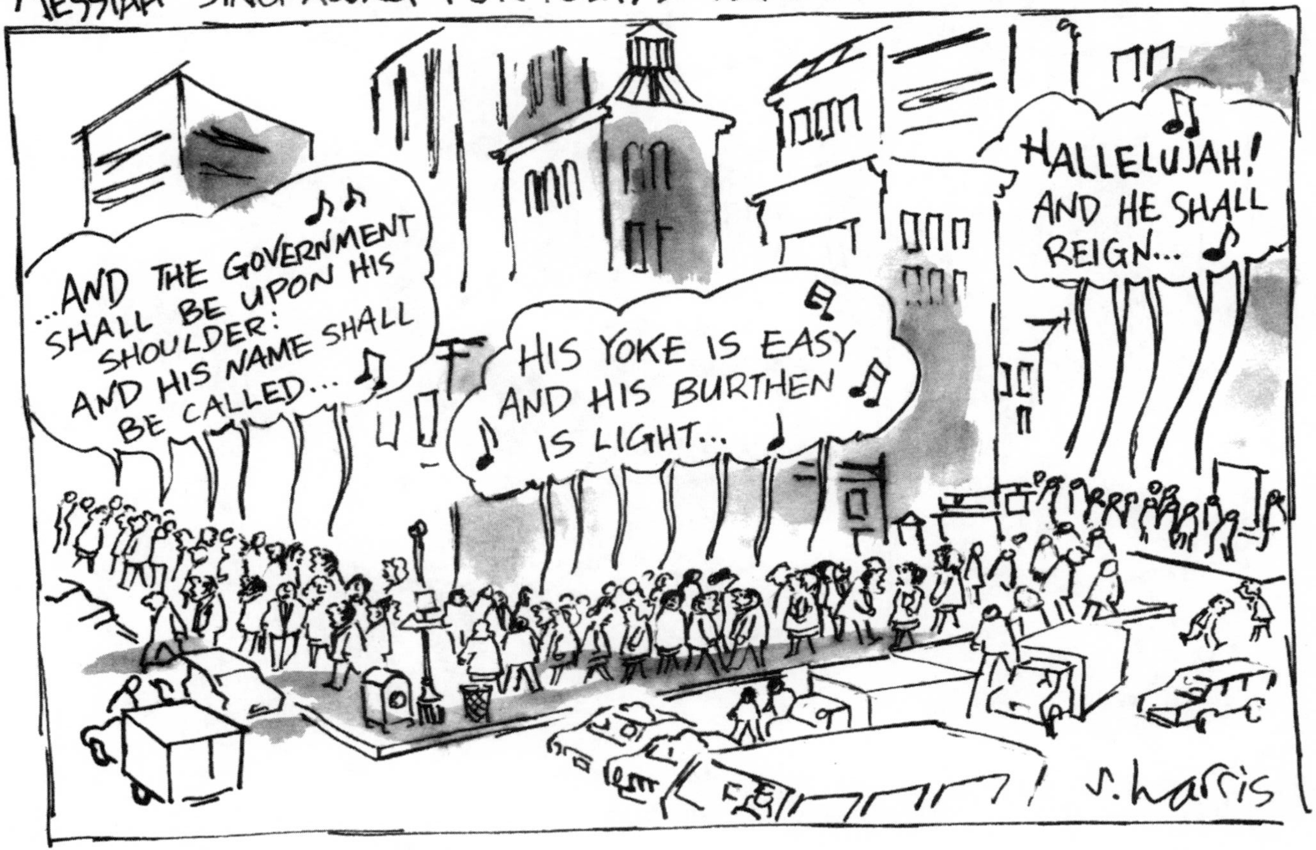

"SURPRISE!"

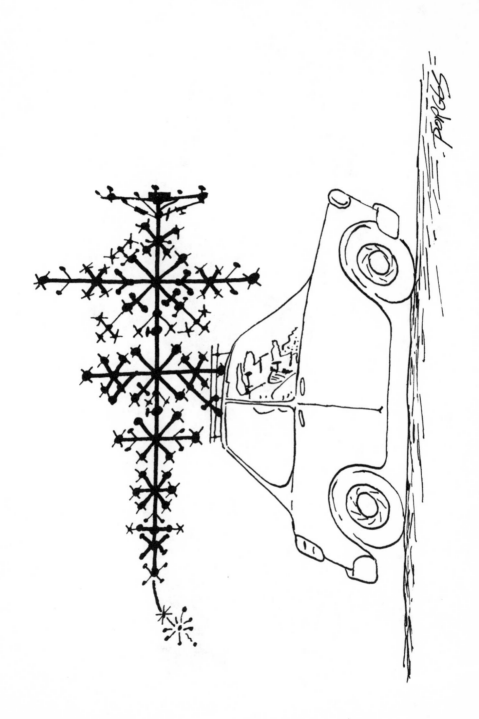

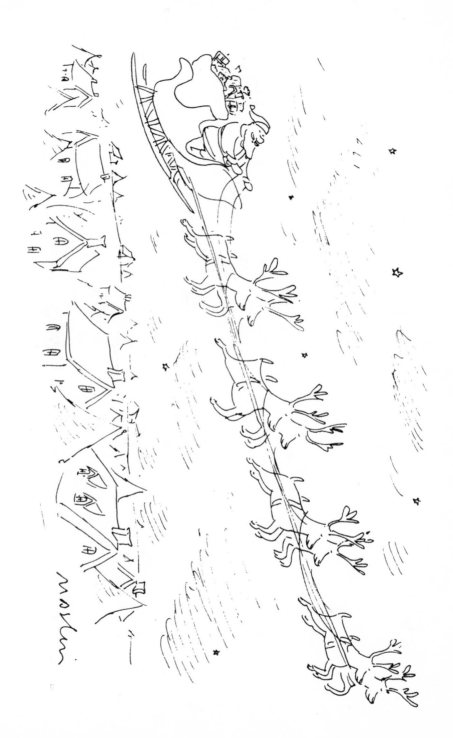

When it definitely, positively has to be there Christmas morning.

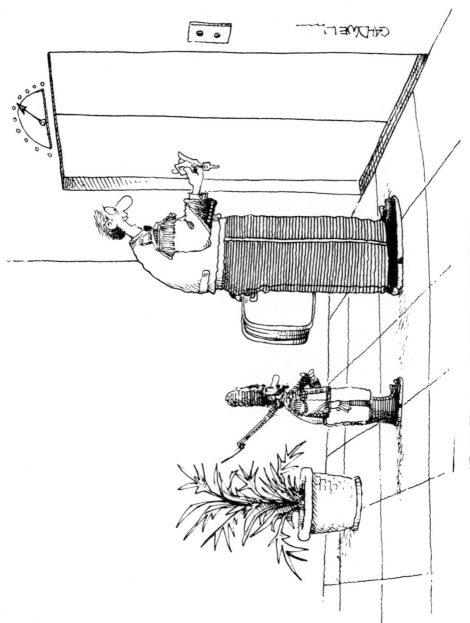

"Room 721, sir. . . .ah yes! The Nutcracker Suite!"

"Yes, Virginia. There is a Santa Claus."

"I can remember when all we needed was someone who could carve and someone who could sew."

"I'm giving everyone I know a kiss and a hug for Christmas and that's all I'm giving them."

"I always fly down and spend the holidays with my children."

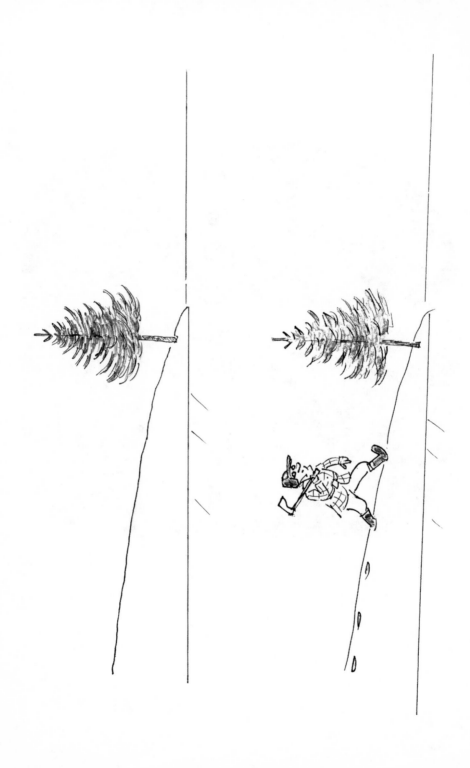

"The trips, the yachts, the oil wells — according to your Christmas newsletter, you folks are in big trouble."

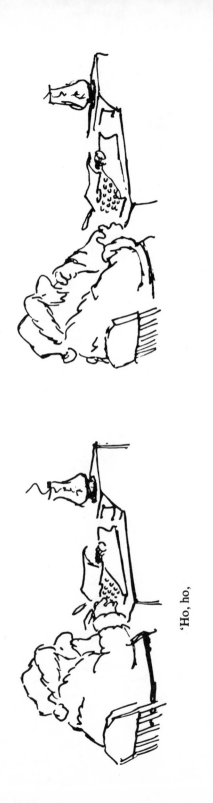

'Ho, ho, ho.'

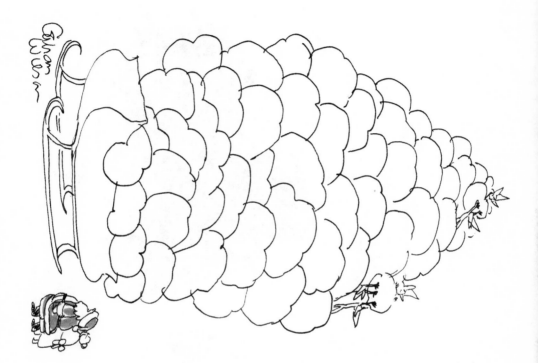

"Remind me next year to set up pick-up points along the way."

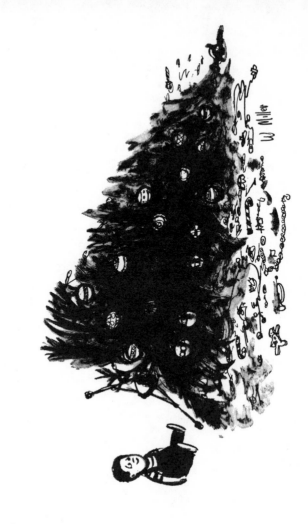

"He said his first word today — 'timber!'"

"I'm doing the thank-you notes, Joseph. Do you remember if Balthazar brought the myrrh or the frankincense?"

THE BIG DRUMMER BOY.

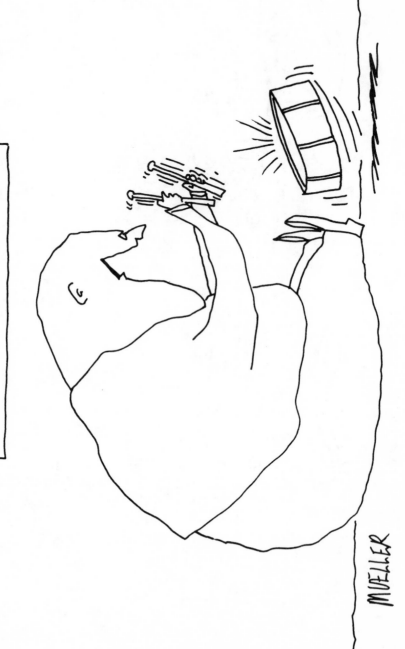

MUELLER

"Let's get someone to snap a picture of you, me, and the tree for next year's card."

"It seems ridiculous to get rid of it now, with Christmas only a couple of months away."

"Mr. Levine, may I see you a moment?"

"Attention — I'm having an endocrinologist in tomorrow to look at all of you."

"Alfred, you may instruct the staff to begin decking the halls."

"Started at 10:15, finished at 10:45 — my Christmas shopping is over!"

"Tonight is catalog night. That's the night each year when our family gathers to drink eggnog, eat fruitcake and throw out the Christmas catalogs."

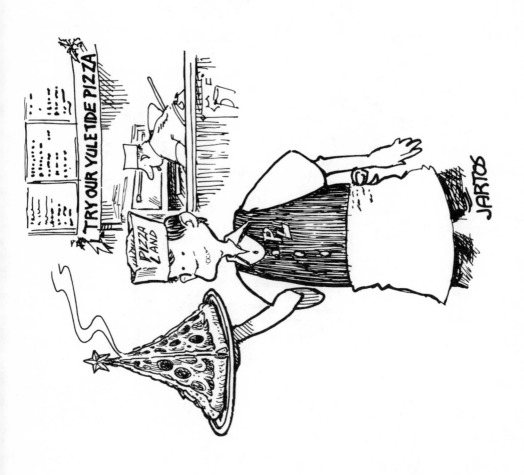

"Camels are all right if you're in a hurry, but we want to make the kid smile."

"Your turn. I kissed her last time."

CHRISTMAS IN FAR-OFF LANDS

SAUDI ARABIA

EVERYONE WAKES UP EARLY, GETS DRESSED, AND GOES TO WORK

INDONESIA

EVERYONE WAKES UP EARLY, GETS DRESSED, AND GOES TO WORK

CHINA

EVERYONE WAKES UP EARLY, GETS DRESSED, AND BIKES TO WORK

"Notice lately how overly religious-oriented
Christmas is becoming?"

"This has been a Christmas when everybody sent us grapefruit."

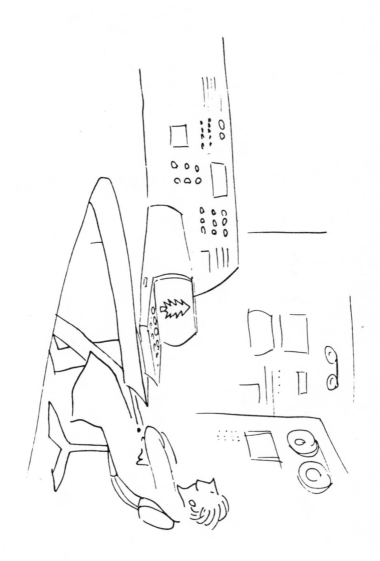

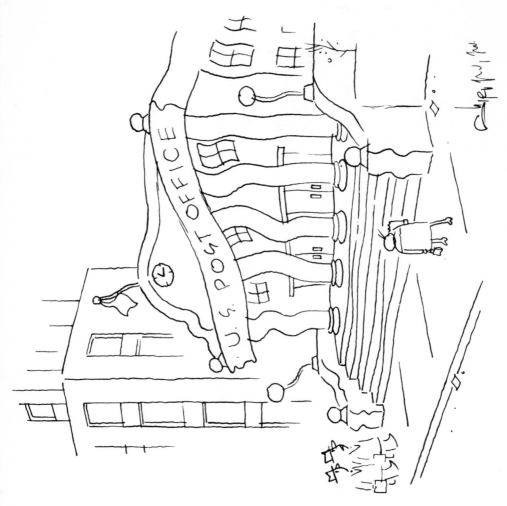

"Post-Christmas let-down, no doubt."

"What she'd really like is a marriage license, but I don't want to spend that much."

"The old man and the reindeers just took off, right?"

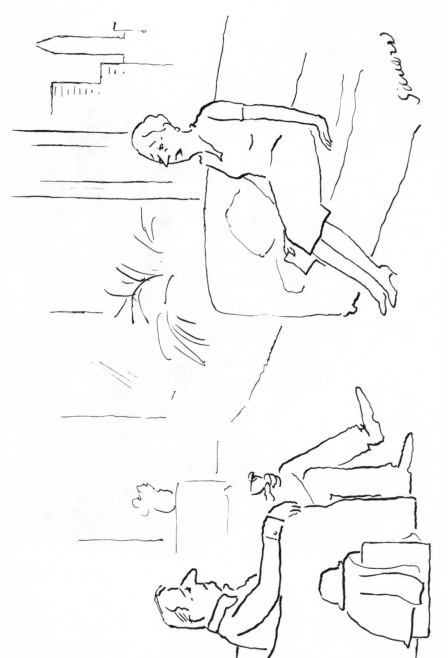

"Here's a gripping modern-day drama. The doorman you didn't tip last Christmas won the lottery, bought the building, and is now going to evict us."

"Dear Santa: How about lunch with me at twelve-thirty on the twentieth at the Princeton Club?"

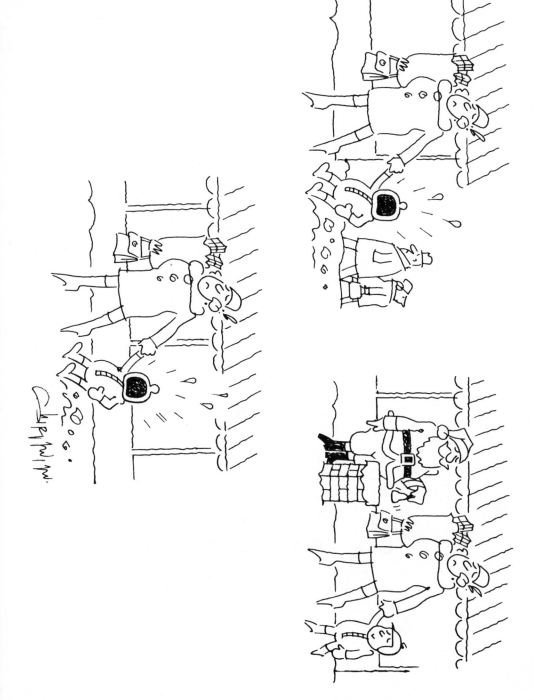

"Here's one from Ted and Gloria. They still haven't realized that we've dropped them."

"Is the North Pole out of town?"

"Do you realize how much trouble I went to to find this for you?"

"Ok. You're the Ghost of Christmas Present.
Quite amusing. Now go away!"

"That puppy made Ralph's Christmas."

"I appreciate the dinner, Cratchit. You have rekindled my belief in the spirit of bachelorhood."

"His cheeks were like roses, his nose like a cherry; his droll little mouth was drawn up like a bow, and the beard on his chin was as white as the snow...."

"How much should I tip him?"

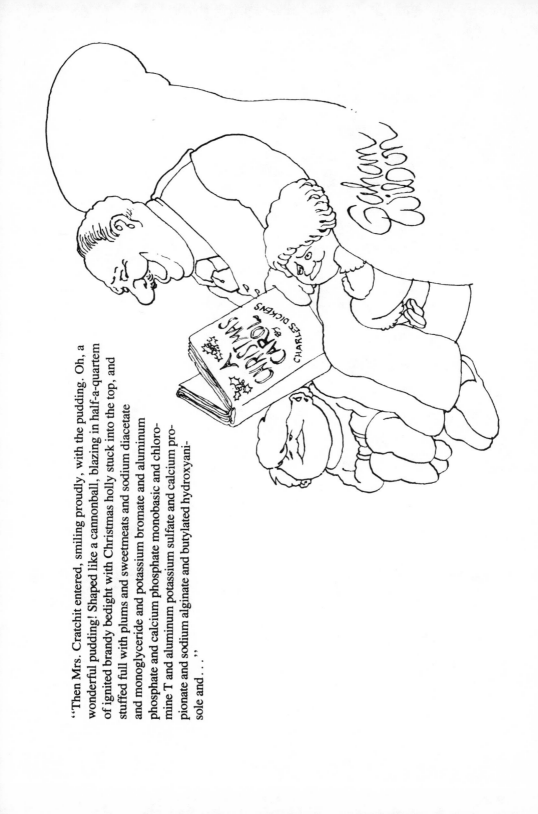

"Then Mrs. Cratchit entered, smiling proudly, with the pudding. Oh, a wonderful pudding! Shaped like a cannonball, blazing in half-a-quartem of ignited brandy bedight with Christmas holly stuck into the top, and stuffed full with plums and sweetmeats and sodium diacetate and monoglyceride and potassium bromate and aluminum phosphate and calcium phosphate monobasic and chloromine T and aluminum potassium sulfate and calcium propionate and sodium alginate and butylated hydroxyanisole and . . ."

"Come on! Can't you see what he's trying to pull?"

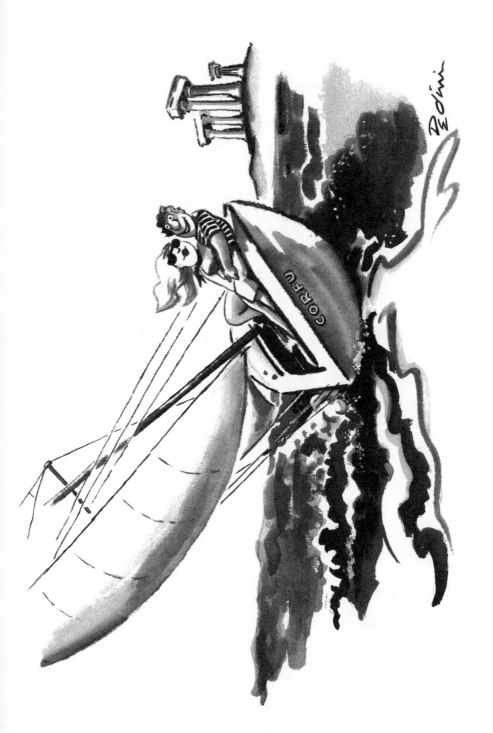

"The beauty of this is that our children have no idea where we've gone for Christmas."

"There are no such things as dancing sugar plums, dear. You just had a bad dream."

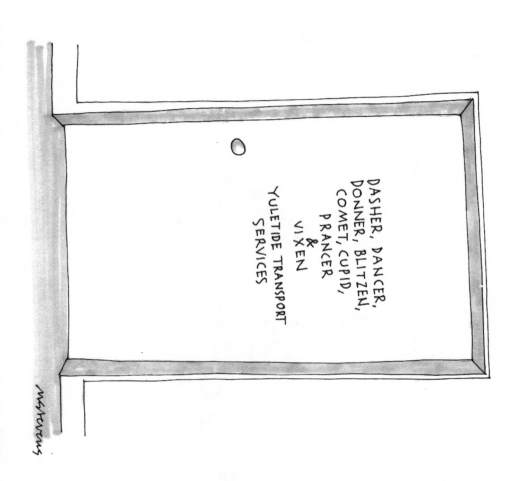

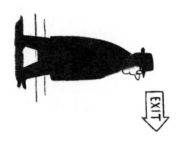

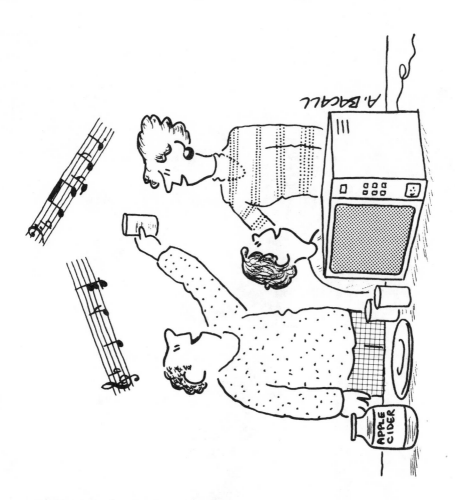

"Chestnuts roasting in a microwave . . . Jack Frost nipping at your nose . . ."

"For god's sake, man, at least take off the suit — there are little children down there!"

"And this time even your precious Superman won't be able to find you! The entire building is lined with fruitcake!!"

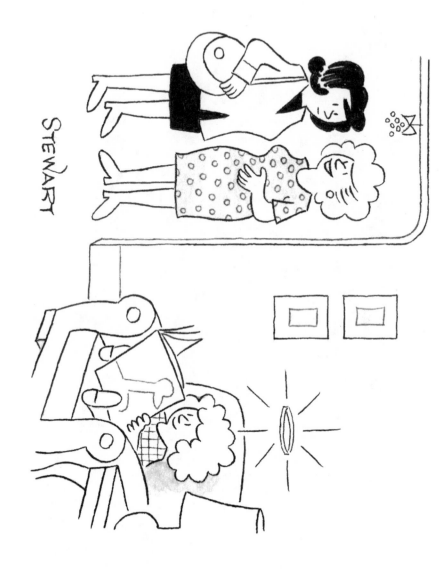

"It appeared in mid-November and I expect it to vanish Christmas morning."

"I already have her main present.
I'm looking for a backup present, just in case."

"I already wrote my letter to Santa Claus for next year and asked him for more track."